LIFE
SWAP

Michaela

LIFE

SWAP

Release Your Past. Accept Your Present.
Create Your Future.

Michaela

Life Swap: Release Your Past, Accept Your
Present, Create Your Future

Library of Congress Cataloging-in-
Publications-Data

Printed in the United States of America

10 9 8 7 6 5 4 3 2 1

Acknowledgements

Dear God: Thank you so much for deeming me worthy. Thank you so much for saving me when I resisted so long. Thank you for your protection even in the risky situations I chose. Thank you for giving me a fresh start and allowing your spirit to freely operate in my life. If you never did another thing for me, I would die in complete gratitude and extremely satisfied. Thank you for being a God of abundance and showing me so much favor. I pray I can fulfill your purpose in this lifetime and everyone, thereafter. Your grace was the difference, and the solution, to all my problems. I cannot thank you enough for inspiring and making possible my Life Swap.

To my amazing fiancé, Chad Thompson: I never in a million years thought I would be blessed with a man as good as you. I just knew the karma of my past would leave me single, or with a man who would never be faithful, and commit to me. Not only are you faithful and committed to me, you prove everyday just how special I am and how much you truly love me. You inspire me to grow and become a greater person everyday through your hard work, dedication, and passion for changing lives around you. Your heart and soul are so beautiful, and I am so honored that you have chosen me to walk beside you and impact the world. Thank you for loving my daughter as your own, and showing her how valuable and powerful she is, even at 4 years old. I cannot wait to bring our baby boy into this world this year. He is so lucky to have you as a dad. I cannot wait to spend my life loving you, supporting you, and building an empire with you. May God always bless our love and help us inspire Life Swaps all around the world.

To my beautiful children, Kaylani and Emir You guys are so special and so loved. Thank you for your beautiful spirits and curious minds. God perfectly created you both and I will always strive to be the best mother I can be and lead you guys into the purpose God placed you here for. May you never forget who you are and whose you are, as I once did. There is no better life than one spiritually grounded in love and compassion. I cannot wait to see how you guys impact this world and experience your own Life Swaps over time. You both will be excellent older siblings to your little brother on the way. My unborn son Croix, you are being born into so much love and we cannot wait to meet you. You were an answered prayer and a great display of mercy from God for your dad and me. We did our own *Life Swap* just to create you.

To my parents, friends, family, and fans: Thank you, for the love, support, and positive impact you have had on my life. I hope to add value to your life and inspire you to make your own Life Swap.

Last but not least, my team! Thank you so much for believing in me and my vision. Thank you for the time, energy, ideas, and resources invested to get us this far. If you want to go fast, they say go alone. If you want to go far, build a loyal team and go together! This is only the beginning and I am grateful to be able to have front row seats to your Life Swaps happening right now!

NAMASTE

A Note From the Author

Thank you so much for choosing my book, although I really believe my book chose you. Regardless of who you are, how old you are, and what you look like, you have experienced things over your lifetime that have shaken you, brought you down to your knees, and really forced you to make a major decision.

The life you are living at this very moment is no doubt a reflection and manifestation of that very decision. Life has a way of challenging us and throwing us into a tailspin when we believe we have it all under control. That has been true in my short life of thirty years. What separates and unites us is how we choose to handle every step of our life. If you are anything like me when you look back at your past, there are moments you wish you would have handled differently. Maybe even some moments you wished never happened. I am here to tell you, those moments have already played their part in your life and it's what you do from this moment forward that will truly change your life, and help you create the life you truly desire.

Whether you are at the lowest point of your life or the highest point of your life, the fact that you are reading this book is a great display you are ready for more and are ready for a big change. What is the secret to change? How are some people able to go through life and not only overcome their obstacles, but experience amazing things and great achievements somewhat effortlessly? The secret is "Life Swap." What is life? Life is the period between birth and death. What is a swap? By definition, it means an act of exchanging one thing for another. In this book, it means: 'Start With A Prayer.'

In this book, I share with you how I swapped my old life of promiscuity and self-destruction for my new life of faith and freedom. When considering all I have been through, and all I have been able to accomplish, it is crystal clear that I made a 180-degree change. But *how*? How was I able to make that transition, break those habits, let go of those people, and even feel worthy of this new sense of life? When pondering that, the Holy Spirit revealed to me the very simple answer— Start With A Prayer. I felt like the greatest light bulb in my life had come on. That was exactly it! Every single problem I overcame, and every opportunity that I have encountered, started with a prayer. It started with me asking God for something. Setting an intention. Expressing a desire. As I became more aware of my true source and power, I started getting better with my questions, and my conversations to God. When I am intentional about my prayers, amazing things happened, and continue to happen. I am not special; you have that power also.

The best thing about prayer is, anyone can do it, and you don't have to be smart, religious, or in a church for it to change your life. As you read this book, and learn more about me and my story, I encourage you to be intentional about your *Life Swap*. What do you want to change about your life? What do you want to be completely different in ninety days? Maybe it's your health; a relationship with spouse, family, or friend; your finances; or even just your mindset. Have a pen and paper handy so you can follow along with the exercises that will help begin to transform your mind. Lastly, remember for the best results you must SWAP (Start With A Prayer) every day, in every situation, for every request. Make the decision to believe that you can truly have the life you desire and ask for it! Let go of the past, accept accountability for your present, and take responsibility for your future. Here is the story of my *Life Swap*.

Introduction

No one wants to be broken.

No one wants to be used and abused.

No one wants to have the sacred, intimate parts of them mishandled during their moments of vulnerability.

No one wants to have the succulence of their innocence sifted from them.

No one *wants* to be in "the life" that I come from.

Over the course of my life, I have encountered many women of all different races and nationalities. They have different social statuses, different beliefs, different thought processes, different values, and so on and so forth. But, one of the common threads that seem to run deep through many of the ones I've met is, their story of brokenness. Regardless to whether they were the wealthy and degreed, or the hardworking woman struggling to make ends meet in order to take care of themselves and their children; the one thing that linked them together making them all the same, was the fact that at some point in their life they had been hurt, abused, and had their heart shattered into pieces for one reason another. However, many of them had learned to pick those pieces up, patch them together, and smile as though they had never been broken. They had somehow learned how to live through it. But even the ones who'd learned how to live through it, were sometimes still not healed and were yet to be WHOLE again—or in their pre-broken state.

My heart weeps each time I come across a broken woman who continues to make decisions that break them repeatedly. See, no one starts out in life broken. You may come from some broken circumstances, but when you are born, regardless to what you are surrounded by, you enter this world with a clean slate. It's not until you live a little bit of your life that people began to chip away at your wholeness. It's not until that first snide comment that gnaws away at your self-esteem that you begin to come apart at the seams. A combination of those sort of disappointments, the buildup of rejection, the loss of loved ones, and the pain from obliterated hearts, cause an once whole and complete person to be anything but.

As I reflect on my own life, and the genesis of my brokenness, I see myself as an innocent little girl being introduced to inappropriate sexual behavior by my favorite uncle, that would birth an insatiable, unhealthy desire for money, power, and sex. An inappropriate encounter that would repeat for what seems like eternity, only to end with this man—who had crossed all sorts of boundaries with me and awaken so many feelings a child should not be feeling—to casually say one day, in the kitchen, before going on a family encounter, "Miki, this thing that we have going on has to stop. I hope Jehovah forgives me and one day you can, too." At the time my very innocent and young self didn't understand what had even happened up until this point. I knew it wasn't right, but it also hadn't entirely registered in my head as bad. Prior to that, encounters would often begin with things like, "I wonder if you will still want me when you are older," or "I know why you wanted to stay home with me today." I loved my Uncle and outside of the inappropriate sexual behavior we had a great relationship and I remember doing many fun things together as a child. From Disney shows to traveling. It wasn't until the inappropriate behavior stopped that I later understood that I had been taken advantage of and sexually abused. I vividly remember at 11 years old sitting inside my Kingdom Hall and hearing a brother say, "Baptism is a way to be made clean again and Jehovah will forgive all your sins." You see, when my uncle said he needed forgiveness from Jehovah, I took that shame and guilt also and felt like I needed that same forgiveness and purifying. So, at 11 years old, I made the decision to get dipped in the water as one of Jehovah's Witnesses and hopefully be made clean of "this thing" my uncle and I had going on. I remember the feeling in my gut walking in that auditorium filled with thousands of people there to bear witness to my public dedication. I knew it wasn't right, but it also didn't register as wrong to me either.

Have you ever faced a situation in your lifetime where the actions taking place or the decisions you were making didn't seem right or wrong to you? That gut feeling telling you that maybe that's not the right thing, place, or person for you, but you justified it as *"well, it's not wrong either"* or *"It's the right thing for me right now."* I have felt it several times in my life. For instance, when my uncle first kissed me; getting baptized as one of Jehovah's Witnesses; Getting married at 18 to a man I wasn't even in a relationship or in love with; and entering the Adult Industry. Every time I ignored my gut instinct and made a temporary life changing decision it had a great impact on my life and triggered some of my greatest Life Swaps.

My first *Life Swap* was beyond my control. Before even understanding what oral sex, fondling, or lust was, as a child, I was thrown into a sick relationship with that trusted family member. The aftermath, as a teenager I became very promiscuous and ultimately that sexual abuse would serve as the catalyst that would catapult me into a life that's often shunned and shamed by morally driven, Bible Belt Christians, and upstanding housewives. And overtime it would also become the reason I would begin a journey of empowering women around the world to become a better version of themselves and create the dream life they desire. As we go on this journey to wholeness, I sincerely hope that by the time you turn the last page; you will have made the commitment to not live life any other way than to your maximum potential. I hope that you will begin to smile again, and not that fake smile you have mastered so no one will see that really you are crying inside. I hope that by the time the last word travels through the obstacle course of your brain, you will feel empowered to live your best life—now. No matter what has happened to you in the past, you are getting ready to shed the weight of it. God's desire for you is to be in good health and prosper, as your soul prospers.

It's been amazing for me to witness and encounter so many women with similar and much more extreme stories than mines completely swap their lives out and create the lives they dreamed of. Lives other people said they would never have. Lives their past never set them up to achieve. Watching other women turn their pain into purpose and their passions into profits triggered me to dig deeper inside myself and make the same thing happen in my own life. I am so grateful for the women that came before me and for God placing them within my reach. What I have also seen, is some of these very same women achieve it all so it seems from the outside and then still feel stuck, unfulfilled, and undesired on the inside. Whether this is your first or multiple time doing a Life Swap, this book is the predestined tool designed to get all your pieces in one place, so we can rebuild you to be the woman you were created you to be. Repeat after me three times: "My past will never return. Today, and forward, I will take accountability for my present and responsibility for my future."

Chapter One

The Origin of Woman

Eve. The first (recorded) woman to exist according to Biblical scholars. A woman with a story that starts out beautiful but quickly takes a turn for the worse. I've heard women say, "It's Eve's fault I'm having all of this labor pain!" This is said, because it is stated that was her curse for being bamboozled by a slick talking serpent. This woman, who is said to be the Mother of mothers, is loved and hated by all women who have had to experience the excruciating pain of childbirth.

According to the Bible, her decision to eat that fruit caused an inherited reaction of pain that would trickle down to women until the end of time. Eve, I suspect, was an Alpha female. I say that because somehow Eve was able to get her husband to sin against God when he knew he was the one placed in charge. Somehow Adam relinquished his authority to his wife, because the Bible tells us that she gave him the fruit, and he without much, if any, hesitation, ate of the fruit as well. Either she had a strong personality or Adam was like most men wanting to please their woman. Perhaps it was the seductiveness of her

voice that made his entire mind leave him—a decision that Bible readers know caused them to be evicted from their home.

But, let's look at Eve and how and why she was created. The first thing I want to point out is that Bible history states that she was taken from Adam's rib. The rib is that one bone in the body that you cannot repair. It must heal on its own. So, Adam was put to sleep, and this beautiful woman, who God created to be his helpmeet, was birthed.

Eve emerged as just what Adam needed. She didn't have to go through any three step programs, or take any classes, to be enough for him. She was the whole package from day one. With that said, I don't know how long they were in the garden before she was drawn away by the serpent, but at some point, something went wrong. I have always wondered how a woman can go from having it all to allowing a stranger, a trespasser, to convince her to put it all in jeopardy. What happened between chapter two and three of the books of Genesis that made this woman sacrifice her household for a piece of fruit? It's not like she was hungry with no food to eat—she had a "house" full of groceries. She had a loving husband who praised her. A lifestyle that she was brought into and didn't have to do anything to maintain it.

What happened to this woman?

The Bible says the serpent was very crafty than any other living creature. So, you mean to tell me that Eve tore up her household because of some charm? Wow. That sort of brings it to perspective, right? Her sole purpose was to be a helpmeet for her husband. Ladies, maybe you can help me with this. What would cause a woman to forfeit such a comfortable life of luxury where her only job was to please her man, for some fruit? And so, I ask you. What have you given up for something that didn't even last? Maybe you had it good at one point, but you made some bad choices that you are still recovering from. If you were to take a ride back down memory lane, I think you would agree that some of the things you got in exchange for your sanity, peace, and comfort was in no way worth it. So, Eve, the woman who started out as whole, became broken in the moment she allowed herself to be tricked. The moment she allowed herself to listen to anything he had to say was the moment it all went South.

Although Eve was punished because of her decision, she didn't die. I know you, yes, you, may have made a string of bad decisions but the bottom line is, and the great part about it is, you didn't die. You are still here. Even though you may have to live with some scars, you are still alive and able to give it your best attempt to get it right. Here is the thing about being broken. For example, if you drop a vase and it in turn becomes broken, even if you patch it up, it's pretty much impossible to put it back together exactly the way that it was. So, the only reasonable thing you can do is take the pieces and build something brand new. And when you really think about it, is there anything wrong with brand new? Would you prefer a new car or a used car? A new dress or a hand me down? A new hair style or a style you've been wearing for the last two years? You get my point? Sometimes new is the best thing that can happen to you.

Eve started out in purpose and ended up in pain. According to Biblical belief, her pain was transferred to the entire female species in that childbirth for women, often believed to be the most excruciating pain there is. Be careful to not make decisions that not only affect you but affect others as well. Don't be the reason that other destinies that are connected to yours are altered because of your wrong decisions going forward. Because you are still here, you are still capable of making better choices. You can't change what was, but you can most definitely decide what will be. So, my friend, what will it be?

Here are three things you can learn from Eve:

1) The importance of staying in the will of God.

2) The importance of not losing your identity no matter what.

3) The importance of maintaining your focus.

Those three things will aid you for the rest of your life in being whole. There is nothing and no one worth being outside of the will of God for your life.

What do I mean by staying in "the will of God? The will of god is the purpose he placed each one of us on this earth for. Each one of us were placed here to contribute to fulfilling God's ultimate plan for humanity. However, the irony of it all is that being in the will of God is also an invitation we must accept and a choice we must decide. The same creator who made earth, animals, humans, and so many other amazing things could have easily forced us all to be uniformed in talent, language, look, and life's experiences. He didn't do that though. He allowed us to have free will. When Eve took the fruit and Adam followed suit, they shifted the paradigm and we were all born into sin. Until we make the decision to submit to the Will of God, we are slaves to our own sinful nature. We make decisions based off our own understanding.

Ultimately, we live a life that's only as big as our eyes can see.

Now before I lose you, I am not saying that you have to kick your boyfriend out, go to church 3x a week, and stop eating bacon to enter the will of God. When I left the Jehovah's Witness faith, I had to navigate my spirituality and what that meant to me. Maybe you also, have been raised with one spiritual culture or lack thereof and have had to or are currently figuring out what and if anything does God mean in your own Adult life.

For me, even though I was raised in a devout household of believers I didn't relate to God and build an intentional relationship until I was about 25 and newly pregnant with my daughter. That's when I really started searching for something different in my life and started praying for these changes. I didn't know if God was listening to me or if he would reward me since I was at the time living a less than Godly lifestyle. To be honest, my life was very scandalous at the time as a full time Adult Entertainment Professional for the past several years. I was desperate for a change and a better way of living and thinking. Without even realizing the shift I was creating in my life, that was my first intentional life swap moment. I started with prayer and asked God to show me a better way. I specifically started pouring out in detail the life I wanted to live. I started pursuing knowledge, relationships, and skills that could bring me closer to this life I was praying for God to show me. This time, I was crazy enough to believe that if God was listening, he was also powerful enough to grant all my wishes.

Staying in the will of God is going to look different for every person and ultimately means not losing sight of serving a greater purpose during your human existence and following the path God places before you. Be bold in your requests and asking God to show you his purpose for you and maximize your potential. You are asking for supernatural blessings and experiences to occur in your life and you are giving up the right to follow your own path and agreeing to be spirit led. Yes, I believe that we were all placed here to do something great but all of us don't achieve that. But, why not? What separates the purpose driven; goal crushing; happy; money making people from the ones that just live ordinary lives often struggling to be positive, enjoy meaningful relationships, or live above middle class and poverty level? It's that one is living in purpose under the will of God and the other is still trying to figure it out on their own strength.

In writing this book, the burning question in my mind, *"How do I achieve the life I want to live?"* was answered. You SWAP one life for another. How do you swap your life? What does that even mean? You start with a prayer. Everything I achieved in life has originated with me praying constantly, learning to hear the answers, and following the spirit I felt inside having faith that it was God responding. You don't have to be religious or go to a building to pray, you just have to do it.

Never forget who you are or whose you are. I'm sure if Eve could do it all over again, she would scream bloody murder at the sight of the serpent. And, I bet, some of you reading this book, would run as fast as Forrest Gump if given the opportunity to resist some of the demons that tripped you up and lose sight of who you are destined to be. I'm certain that at the sight of some people right now, or the thought of some situations, you cringe because you remember how stupid it was to risk your life and sanity. Once more, you can't change the past, but you can direct your future. And what we know to be a fact is that the will of God is the safest place to be.

Next, don't lose who you are, trying to be who someone else wants you to be. Eve knew who she was. She had no doubt about who she belonged to. But the smooth-talking serpent made her forget what she KNEW. That's one of the greatest tragedies about that situation. The enemy made her forget what she KNEW to be true. How sad would it be to fail a one question test when you KNOW the answer? If I asked you what one plus one equals, more than likely, you would not hesitate in answering with the number two. Why? Because you KNOW that's the answer. How easy would it be for someone to ask you that same question and convince you that perhaps what you thought you KNEW is now speculative and there could be another answer? Not easy at all, huh? Of course not. You have been taught your entire life the answer to that question. Well, Eve, from her beginning days on Earth, was taught by her husband that they were to not touch, let alone, eat from the tree of knowledge. We all know that Eve had shown up for class and had comprehended what her husband taught her, because when the enemy first tried her, she recited back to him the teaching she'd gotten. Somehow, he was able to convince her that one plus one didn't equal two, and what she KNEW, she really didn't know. What a travesty that is. Listen, you can never allow the enemy to trick you out of knowing what you know. Maybe you have already been tricked and you are saying to yourself, "Michaela, I don't know who I am anymore, or I am still trying to figure it out". I am here to tell you if you don't know in your mind, you were born knowing it in your spirit. You know who God says you are. You know what you are capable of. You know that the plan for your life is to give you a wonderful future. You know that His promises are yes and amen. You know that above all things God wants you to prosper and be in good health. That's what you KNOW. So, keep what you KNOW in the forefront of your mind so that you don't lose your identity when in fact you KNOW who you are.

Last, don't lose your focus. Distractions are going to come if you continue to live. There'll never be an instance where you'll sail through life, reach your goals or fulfill your dreams, without some sort of obstacle trying to hinder you. But you overcome these obstacles by keeping your eyes focused on the end goal. In Eve's case, she lost her focus the moment she entertained what the enemy had to say. Because unless she was accustomed to serpents talking, then why would she bother to speak to something beneath her? Herein lies an even greater point.

Don't ever allow something beneath you to take away your focus. I mean nothing should take your focus, but especially not anything beneath you. You are too valuable to this Earth and your purpose is greater than you. Distractions cause you to prolong getting to your destiny. For years, I allowed my past experiences as a child to shape how I thought and how I made decisions as an Adult. I got so distracted with the luxury and earning six figures that I lost focus of wanting to help other little girls and women or become something bigger than what I experienced. I wonder how God feels knowing He has planned this great and wonderful future for us, but we prolong getting there with our bad choices? How frustrating it must be to watch us struggle to get there when all we have to do is stay in His will, maintain who we are and what we know, and keep our focus. Trust me, I'm the first to say that I know it's easier said than done. It's not the simplest thing to do those three things, but at some point, be it simple or difficult, you have to make up in your mind that where you are going is more important than some enticing offer from the enemy. You've got to decide within yourself that you'd rather obey God than suffer the consequences. You must be determined that no matter what come and who goes, your only desire is to be pleasing to God and fulfilling your purpose. Nothing else matters. Don't be one of those people who wait until the very end of their life to make peace with their past. Decide to make the changes necessary right now, so the rest of your life can be the absolute best of your life.

Self-Reflection

1) What distractions have you allowed?

_____

_____

_____

_____

_____

_____

_____

2) How did those distractions alter your thoughts about yourself?

_____

_____

_____

_____

_____

_____

_____

3) How did those distractions alter your life?

_____

_____

_____

_____

4) What did you learn from the distractions?

_____
_____
_____
_____
_____

5) How do you plan to prevent yourself from being distracted?

_____
_____
_____
_____
_____

Chapter Two

Laughing Is the New Crying

Nothing grieves me more than seeing a woman cry any other tears than tears of joy. Her tears are indicators that in some area she has been broken. She has been hurt. Abused. Misused. Rejected. Oppressed. Forgotten about. Her tears are an indicator that her heart has gotten too full, and the only way she can deal with the pain, the frustration, the brokenness, is to cry. But, most of the time, a woman cries alone. She is more inclined to cover her tear stained face with makeup and a smile.

Many women who have been hurt in any way, contribute it to a man. Very few blame their discontentment with their life on a woman unless the blame is placed on her mother. And, for that ladies, I want to say to you I'm sorry. I'm sorry for all the hurt that you've had to experience in your life. But, can I say this to you? You don't have to hold on to that hurt and bitterness. You don't have to continue to digest the pain someone caused you. You can learn to let it go.

I've discovered that laughing is the new crying. So many people are hiding behind their infectious laugh, and people are believing they are fine simply because their smile lights up the room. But I'm learning to look deeper and beyond a person's comedic nature, because case in point; Robin Williams, who spent much of his life making us laugh, took his own life because he was no longer able to make himself laugh.

Mental health is something rarely discussed but it is a much needed and necessary conversation to have for the sake of those who have mastered living for others and not themselves. For you to be completely whole, you have to have a strong mind. I am not one of those people who preach and promote you going to church, but not going to counseling or finding someone to confide in when you have had devastating and traumatic events to occur in your life can be detrimental. I probably would have taken my own life if it were not

Page | 36

for my best friend, Candace. We met when I was 10 years old, and after my sexual abuse had recently ended. I can recall times where I would just spend our sleepovers crying uncontrollably, and she would console me. Or the time where she threatened to tell my mom about my eating disorder if I didn't tell her first. She was the first angel on earth God sent me that I can remember. Sometimes, you don't need another prayer, sometimes a hug will suffice. Sometimes, you just need to hear someone say they are proud of you.

There is a popular story of a married couple who had been trying to conceive a child for a very long time. Matter of fact, they were approaching a hundred years old, and by all accounts, their ability to conceive and deliver a child seemed to be far reaching. So far reaching, that Sarah, the wife, gave her husband to a much younger woman so that he might have a son. Well, even in her doing that, it still did not satisfy the longing she had in her heart to conceive her own child. This was evident because when Abraham, the husband, began to spend time with his child and the child's mother, Hagar, Sarah got upset. She found reason to gripe about Hagar, when in fact it was her bold idea to have this arrangement anyway. I don't believe Sarah was upset with the demands of Hagar, or Abraham's willingness to fulfill her demands.

I believe Sarah was upset because she had convinced herself that she was fine with another woman having her husband's child, and not she herself. I think she had convinced herself that it did not matter if she had lived a life having borne no kids even though at that time that was the stamp of a woman. I think she had convinced herself that although she had spent many days and nights praying, asking, and believing that God was going to answer her prayer; she was disappointed that He had not. So, here this woman was standing on the shores of depression looking out into a sea of possibility. Caught between a tear and a smile. Caught between laughing and crying.

If you have read the story, then you know it ends in her favor. She gets the son she has always prayed for and whatever issue she has with the other woman is resolved. I wonder how many of you can relate to Sarah. How many of you can relate to wanting and desiring something so much, and when it doesn't come, you give up hope? How many of you have had something happen to you that made you convince yourself that your happiness was no longer worth fighting for? Matter of fact, have you convinced yourself that YOU are no longer worth fighting for? That your excitement isn't worth fighting for? That your joy isn't worth fighting for? Who am I talking to? You may be asking yourself how you are supposed to go about reclaiming your joy. How you go about turning that artificial smile into an authentic one.

Well, for starters, as you are reading this book, just know that I believe that some of your heart's desires are going to be met and your faith in yourself will be restored. It may not be what you want to hear, but you are going to have to believe again. Nothing reactivates faith but faith. You have to find a way to hope again. I know it's hard to hope when hope has been deferred. But you make yourself sicker and more frustrated when you choose to defy what comes naturally, and that is to believe. Yes, it's easier for you to believe than it is for you to not. So, what do I want you to do to get that smile back on your face? BELIEVE! Believe that your life is getting better.

Believe that problem has already worked out.

Believe that the situation has a solution.

Believe that your heart won't be broken again. Believe that your children will be just fine.

Believe that God is going to take care of you.

Believe that the rest of your life will be the best of your life.

Believe, believe, believe! And I can assure you that once your faith kicks back into action, the true, genuine smile you once wore but was faded by the pressures of life, will return. And those tears of sorrow will be replaced by tears of joy. Do you believe that with me today?

I want you to speak the following affirmation every morning and then I want you to write your own.

Positive Affirmation

I am beautiful and wonderfully made. I lack nothing. I am equipped with what I need to be the best version of myself.

Chapter Three

You're Worthy

Worthy. What does that word really mean? By definition, it means "having or showing the qualities or abilities that merit recognition in a specified way." I can think of many times in my life dating back to early childhood throughout my early 20's when I didn't feel "worthy." From being bullied as a schoolgirl for having big hair to after the countless times I've done the walk of shame after trading my body, energy, and time for money and a false sense of power. I know what it feels like to have to try and hold your head up as you're walking away with the bag secured or connection made, but inside dealing with the insecurity that comes with the process of getting there.

Most women have seen the movie, "Pretty Woman." I'd bet that it's one of the most favorite movies of women, of all time. It surely cannot be debated that it's a classic. But what is it about this story of a woman, who's by society's definition is a prostitute, that we love so much? Why do we grab our popcorn, glasses of wine, and make our husbands, or significant others, watch Julia Roberts character go down on Richard Gere? What makes us cheer her on as she's strolling down Rodeo Drive in Beverly Hills with tons of bags filled with purchases with money, she'd earned from sleeping with the wealthy tycoon? We swoon over their unlikely Hollywood romance and then our hearts dive into our feet when it appears, they will part ways without their happily ever after.

So, why is this? Why do we watch and accept this? Women across the world have secretly wished they could have a similar chance meeting with a wealthy guy. But, for most, it will never happen. However, for about forty million, they live their lives everyday just like Julia Roberts' character— as an adult industry professional or as some would call it, a sex worker.

Havocscope, a provider of data on the black market, in a 2015 book titled Prostitution: Prices and Statistics of the Global Sex Trade, wrote: "Over $180 billion is spent each year on the global sex trade, with over 10 million women providing services as prostitutes. Some are forced into the trade due to human traffickers, while others enter the trade due to financial hardships or because they think it's a fun and easy way to make money. But, for more than 90% its simply because they haven't healed from emotional and sexual trauma." Social media has made this lifestyle much more public in recent years. From the street level prostitute that's addicted to drugs to the high end beautiful girl that makes a fortune and lives like a princess capitalizing off her charm and good looks there is a steady incline of more women, and men, entering into the lifestyle for one reason or another. Even media and many songs glorify women trading their looks and bodies for financial gain. However, there is a large group of these women living in our subdivisions, running our favorite companies, picking up their kids from the same school, and overall living quiet and discrete double lives.

As I said before, being in this line of work comes with guilt and the shame because the industry is not created equal when it comes to labeling what's considered to be gainful employment. Let's face it. Most of us work for the same reason. To afford the lifestyle we have, to provide for our families, and to build, and leave a legacy for the generations who come after us. However, due to the criminalization of the sex worker and the perception given by media, our world creates a narrative that will more than likely never change, unless women (and men) who have been involved in this life, change it. The world can forgive a drug dealer, gang member, and perhaps even murderer.

However, the woman who has sold herself for money is often judged and shamed before any mercy is shown. Therefore, so many people with this past hide from it and mute themselves from sharing it once they escape. It took me a long time to be willing to confess this to the world about my own life, but there are too many women who are stuck that need to see that they are not trash and deserve everything the next woman does. Your past decisions do not have to permanently dictate your future outcomes.

I will admit that it took years for me to deem myself worthy of a new life and a new love after leaving the lifestyle. I sometimes sit and reflect on my blessings and the journey that led to where I am now. Just a few years ago, you wouldn't have been able to convince me that I would be a housewife, with a loving fiancé, two beautiful children (with one on the way), a thriving business life, and an author who's soon to be known across the country. No. I didn't think I would be living a bad life, because my life in the adult industry afforded me a very luxurious lifestyle. But I wasn't mentally wealthy. What do I mean by that? See, there's a difference in having physical things that make you happy and having a healthy quality of life that makes you happy in every area of your life. When you're mentally healthy it's much easier to recognize the power, you have to shape the life you want to live.

This chapter is for those who have decided that because you've been labeled adversely by society, you feel contrite. Listen, my loves, you are worthy of every good thing that can happen to anyone with any background. Yes, your past may be a little colorful and it may sometimes plague you from seeing that your future can contain even more colors; but it's not too late and all hope is not lost. And, no, you don't have to change the things you may think in order to get those things. Just your mindset and your daily actions.

There are three phases to a life swap:

1. The Awakening Phase:

Your acknowledgement that your life as it currently is cannot continue, and a drastic change is essential for your survival.

2. The Double Life Phase: This is a time where you may be caught between your old life and the new life you are created.

3. The Arrival Phase: You have successfully created a new life, fully replacing that thing you wanted to swap out.

As I mentioned earlier the arrival of my daughter is what really triggered my awakening. I just didn't want to repeat what I saw my family do. I wanted to set a new standard for her. However, I remember being torn in between two worlds for a very long time. The Double Life Phase can be the most difficult one to transition from and where many people just give up and stay stuck in their past and present life. However, I did the mental work required and started taking the steps to create my life on the other side until I created a pathway out physically. I couldn't just walk out of my six-figure career overnight and automatically know everything I needed to start a business, have a healthy relationship with a man, or change my life. I could however start learning and applying what I learned. There are many reasons why you may have to stay in your circumstances past your awakening, but you can change your mind set at any time you choose. My love, I promise you that once your mindset changes, it won't be long before your reality transforms also. A powerful woman once affirmed, *"All my dreams and goals are coming into my reality, how they get done is not my business but God's business."* You have to believe that everything can change for you just as much as you believe you will wake up tomorrow.

One of the things that come along with working in the adult industry or even just being a woman in today's age is often a woman feeling the need to do enhancements to herself in order to compete. I support a woman doing whatever she desires to do in order to be happy, but I want to address the woman who feels she must do those things in order to be accepted by society or earn more income. I applaud women who are comfortable in their skin and who have decided that it doesn't matter who likes it, or who doesn't, if they are healthy, they are alright with what they have or what they purchase. Confidence is sexier than any surgical enhancement. While in my former life I was not the "vixen" type, I earned far more than a lot of my vixen colleagues. After retiring, I did choose to get enhancements done, but doing it because it solely was what I wanted and not for someone else or the industry pressure felt GREAT!

We can all use some improvement in some areas in our lives. But what I am saying is, know your worth. Know who God says you are. Know how valuable you are to any person who is privileged to have you in their life. You may be single right now and feel as though nobody wants you, or that you have to alter yourself so that someone will want you. Maybe you have even felt like acting out and making careless choices out of pain. Stop thinking like that. You will meet the right person and the right person will love you as you are and will be willing to work with you in bettering yourself. Beauty, you are worthy of a love that is so pure that it almost feels like Heaven on Earth. That love must first come from you towards yourself.

The notion that you have to be accepted is instilled into us as a child and is carried over into your mindset as an adult. But you are no longer in high school trying to be in the popular club. You don't have to do out of the ordinary things for the sake of attention. You don't have to go out of your way and overextend yourself just for people to welcome you into their clique. Find freedom in being yourself. Find freedom in knowing that people are blessed to have you in their life. Find freedom in accepting and embracing your personality and I promise you there are people in this world who will meet you and wonder where you've been all their life.

If you are struggling with low self – esteem, I want you to identify the reasons why. Figure out and pinpoint the exact moment you realized, or should I say convinced yourself, that you were not perfect, and deal with that one moment. Afterwards, deal with every subsequent moment that came after that contributed to the frosted vision you have of yourself. Yes, go back and deal with it. You can't change your perspective of yourself until you first determine how that perspective was formulated in the first place. In other words, get to the root of where it all began so you can pluck it up from the root, and begin a whole new way of thinking. For some of you it may help to do some daily affirmations. Sometimes we have to encourage ourselves and speak to our inner person so that we can build ourselves back up in the places we have been torn down. I remember I used to think I had to do favors for men to show my appreciation for them or have their love. That was rooted in my inappropriate relationship with my uncle and possibly even not having a strong emotional connection to my own father. I had to work through this and convince myself that I was worth so much more. I had to learn and build my value outside of my looks, charm, and body. Some things you need to tell yourself daily are: *"I was created to live a happy and prosperous life." "I am beautiful." "I am worthy." "I was worth saving." "I deserve to be used as a vessel to fulfill God's will." "I love myself and the people in my life love me, too."* Those are just examples.

Take the space below to write in your own affirmations and declare them over your life daily. Don't allow anyone, or anything, the power or opportunity to steal another day of your joy, peace, and self-love.

_____

_____

_____

_____

_____

_____

_____

_____

_____

_____

_____

_____

_____

_____

_____

_____

Chapter Four

Finding Purpose In Pain

In the famous words of Langston Hughes, "Life for me ain't been no crystal stare."

I think many people can relate to those words. For the most part, we have all been dealt some hands in life that shook us to the core. We have all been dealt some hands in life that had us trying to figure out if we were going to lose our mind. We have all been dealt some hands in life that left us tethering along the edges of depression and saneness.

But, if you are reading this book, somehow you made it to this point. The difference between a winner and a quitter is simple. One keeps going. When you experience the devastating pain of something, there is one part of you that tries to talk you into giving up on life, your dreams, your hope, and your goals. Then, there is the other side of you that tries to convince you that you have no other choice but to get up and move forward. That part of you is the part that you must continually feed because it is impossible to live life absent from any sort of pain. The pain isn't what kills a person, the response to the pain will be the determining factor if you succeed or fail, live or die. And, I want you to always respond to the pain in a manner that puts you in control of the pain. Why? Because pain doesn't have to control you. It only controls you when you allow it. Sometimes pain will blind you of your purpose. But it is imperative that you look deep within the creases of pain and find it anyway. I can guarantee that you can find something positive, productive, and purposeful in every ounce of pain that has wreaked havoc in your life. Not only can you find positivity, productiveness, and purpose, you can find profit. Isaiah 61:7 states that you will get double for your trouble.

In other words, with your trouble comes increase. How does that sound? If you can, imagine all the trouble you have gone through and add up what you are owed because of it. Are you seeing it yet?

I can recall when I was a teenager and internally dealing with trying to process my childhood abuse. The pain was blinding. I became very self-destructive, struggled with an eating disorder, and even attempted to take my own life. Even more so after sharing my secret with family, and my abuser, even being confronted to only deny the truth. I let this pain fester in my soul and replay in my head day after day, year after year. As I got older, I stopped feeling sorry for myself and I let that pain grow into a reckless and immoral lifestyle. I craved control of my sexuality and to have power over my male counterpart. It was a lifestyle where I entered broken and unsure of my dealings with men. Over time I learned more about myself, and I developed a power over them using my charm, body, and wit.

This time my body was not someone's personal playground without my consent, but I was the puppet master orchestrating the encounters for my own gain.

I fell in love with the power, and not to mention the money I would bring in for the almost four years I spent in the adult world. The pain was in control. All I was focusing on was pleasure and how much I could gain. I thank God that He stepped in when He did and shifted something inside my soul that made me only see my escape in His mercy.

I remember going to a Buddhist Temple in Fort Lauderdale, Florida that was operating out of an old tire shop, and just sitting there in a silent room with people from all walks in life learning the power of meditation. That was the first moment of silence I had truly had in a long time. No cheating boyfriend who I was hanging on to at this point only out of familiarity and convenience; no client phone or appointments that had at this point controlled my entire life and schedule; no thoughts of why my favorite uncle who I believed cared for me would use me for his own selfish needs; no questions of how my parents could put my fate in the hands of a religion and not protect, or fight for me to greater extents.

In that moment of silence, I only felt my need for a relief and complete life change. That moment was the day I decided to stop trying to pick up the broken pieces and start completely new. Like a new alias that I would create to attract a new clientele, only this time I would create a completely new person that I was silly and desperate enough to believe would attract a completely new life. I had gotten my first moment of relief. This is the moment I decided to believe in a power that was bigger than my own will. This is when I began to dabble into prayer and the law of attraction, it would be another year before I completely surrendered.

I want you to write down the things that have hurt you the most. Once you have done that, write down what hurt you the most about those things. And, then, I want you to list the positive things that have since come from that hurt, and finally, over in another category, figure out businesses, and services that you can offer from those things.

_____

_____

_____

_____

_____

_____

_____

_____

_____

_____

_____

_____

_____

_____

_____

_____

_____

_____

_____

_____

How many things did you come up with that were income producing? See how a different perspective can cause you to stumble up on your purpose? See, the pain never comes without a reason. Most people just suck it up and figure out a way to live through it. But, when you find the purpose for the pain, you don't have to just live through it, you can live beyond it and be fulfilled while doing so.

The beauty of a single pearl, or a string of the precious stones, is unmistakable. Few jewels capture the eye quite like a perfect pearl. Know how the pearl came to be? In the beginning, it's only a grain of sand. That tiny little irritant slips inside the tight seal of an oyster's shell, and immediately causes discomfort. With no way to expel the grain of sand, with no way to ease the pain, the oyster coats the sand with a layer of the inner lining of its shell to make the sand smooth.

This still does not ease the oyster's suffering. Again, and again the oyster coats the sand, but all the attempts to get rid of the irritant have little effect. As far as an oyster is concerned, what we call a "pearl" is nothing more than great suffering. But one day the oyster is fished from the water and opened. The gem inside has amazing beauty and holds great value – all because the oyster had great suffering. I love this quote: *"All the world is full of suffering. It is also full of overcoming."*–Helen Keller

What makes some people more resilient than others? According to the American Psychological Association resilience is simply adapting well to adversity, tragedy or trauma – something that any of us can work toward. Those who recognize that the struggle is a steppingstone to what lies ahead and who can relinquish control have a stronger ability to bounce back from the bad.

She may be one of the most successful women in the world today, but Oprah worked through incredibly tough demons to arrive here at her current post. She suffered sexual abuse from several family members starting at age 10, which ultimately led to her sexual promiscuity as a teenager. At 14, she became pregnant, but lost her baby boy soon after giving birth. She harbored this painful secret for years until a relative shared her story with the press in 1990. "I soon realized that having the secret out was liberating," she wrote, according to the New York Post. "What I learned for sure was that holding the shame was the greatest burden of all."

Despite the trauma, Oprah was an honors student in high school, earned a full scholarship for college, and is now a woman that millions look up to and admire.

I could list so many stories of success that people have now after having survived tumultuous times. But I want you to focus on your own story.

Take the space on the next page to write your story. Here is the beautiful thing about life. You get to determine how your story ends. So, I ask you, how will your story end? Be bold, dream big, and really visualize everything working out in your favor. Now write it down.

My Memoir

_____

_____

_____

_____

_____

_____

_____

_____

_____

_____

_____

_____

_____

_____

_____

_____

_____

_____

_____

_____

_____

Chapter Five

More Than A Sex Toy

Unfortunately, there are some little boys disguised as men who see women as nothing more than a body for pleasure and companionship or whom they can release their seed in but toss them out like yesterday's trash once the seed manifests into a request for a deeper commitment or even bigger eighteen years of responsibility. A real man will be attracted to you without using your body as his pleasure playground. If you are his wife, then your body somewhat belongs to him, but if not, then you need to let these little boys know that in order to get that privilege a commitment needs to be made with actions. I think Beyoncé says in a song, "If you like it then you need to put a ring on it." Set the standard and stick to it. You are worth more than a casual fling or a baby with no family.

Somewhere down through the generations someone said that our greatest power was between our legs. Even I once believed in "The Power of The Pussy" That is a lie. After a while, what's between your legs is no different from what's between the next woman's legs. Men who are not regenerated in their mind and way of thinking, will see you the same way as he sees the next woman. Unless a man has invested emotions into you, your sex is no different from any other sex he's had. Your greatest weapon is in fact between your ears. It's your mind. How you think. How you process things. A woman's mind and wit can stop a powerful man in his tracks, the same way her body can. Which would you rather use to stop a man? Your mind or your body? Towards the end of my career, I stopped working and began to more casually begin dating very wealthy men. I quickly learned that it took a lot more than great looks to capture and keep a man of influence. Men who have went the distance in their own success want a woman who has value to offer beyond the bedroom. Being culturally aware, well-traveled, and having a strong vision for your own future will attract a man worthy of your time. True power is when you are confident in how beautiful, valuable, and worthy you are and can also respect and honor the beauty and value in someone else. Nothing is sexier than a woman who loves herself being able to project that energy outwards. The more you love and develop yourself the more you open the universe to sending you a man who loves you and will invest in you that much and more.

In the Bible, there's a story of a woman by the name of Rahab. Rahab was a prostitute and for the most part, it's safe to say that at some point that is all she thought she would ever be. Have you ever felt like that? Felt like the most value you had was in how good you were in bed? However, Rahab must have at some point also believed that she was not good at anything else that could make her money. She must have believed that selling her body and allowing men to rent her for the night was the only way she could survive and make ends meet. I'm certain that she had been degraded so much that she threw away the notion that she was good enough to do something else, something that didn't require her to sell herself short for a few dollars and a good time.

The reason I believe this is because when she had an opportunity to use her skills to do something else, she did. Let's look at her story.

""Joshua son of Nun secretly sent out from Shittim two men as spies: "Go. Look over the land. Check out Jericho." They left and arrived at the house of a harlot named Rahab and stayed there. The king of Jericho was told, "We've just learned that men arrived tonight to spy out the land. They're from the People of Israel." The king of Jericho sent word to Rahab: "Bring out the men who came to you to stay the night in your house. They're spies; they've come to spy out the whole country." The woman had taken the two men and hidden them. She said, "Yes, two men did come to me, but I didn't know where they'd come from. At dark, when the gate was about to be shut, the men left. But I have no idea where they went. Hurry up! Chase them—you can still catch them!" (She had actually taken them up on the roof and hidden them under the stalks of flax that were spread out for her on the roof.) So, the men set chase down the Jordan road toward the fords. As soon as they were gone, the gate was shut.

Before the spies were down for the night, the woman came up to them on the roof and said, "I know that GOD has given you the land. We're all afraid. Everyone in *the country feels hopeless. We heard how GOD dried up the waters of the Red Sea before you when you left Egypt, and what he did to the two Amorite kings east of the Jordan, Sihon and Og, whom you put under a holy curse and destroyed. We heard it and our hearts sank. We all had the wind knocked out of us. And all because of you, you and GOD, your God, God of the heavens above and God of the earth below.*

"Now promise me by GOD. I showed you mercy; now show my family mercy. And give me some tangible proof, a guarantee of life for my father and mother, my brothers and sisters—everyone connected with my family. Save our souls from death!" "Our lives for yours!" said the men. "But don't tell anyone our business. When GOD turns this land over to us, we'll do right by you in loyal mercy." She lowered them down out a window with a rope because her

house was on the city wall to the outside. She told them, "Run for the hills so your pursuers won't find you. Hide out for three days and give your pursuers time to return. Then get on your way."

The men told her, "In order to keep this oath you made us swear, here is what you must do: Hang this red rope out the window through which you let us down and gather your entire family with you in your house—father, mother, brothers, and sisters. Anyone who goes out the doors of your house into the street and is killed, it's his own fault—we aren't responsible. But for everyone within the house we take full responsibility. If anyone lays a hand on one of them, it's our fault. But if you tell anyone of our business here, the oath you made us swear is canceled—we're no longer responsible."

She said, "If that's what you say, that's the way it is," and sent them off. They left and she hung the red rope out the window."
Joshua 2:1-21 MSG

Rehab was a master negotiator! The girl had skills. She brokered a deal that would later save her life and the lives of her family. Now, I don't know what happened the night before when the men first arrived at her house, but assuming that they knew she was a harlot, I'm assuming this started out as a business relationship with the two of them being clients just as the others who frequently visited her home. To them, she may have just been a good time the night before, but to her she was the one designated to save her family. They quickly learned that whatever they paid her to do, if anything, that she was more than just a sex toy. She was also their rescuer. She apparently was good with design because she was also able to hide them on the roof under flax that the Bible says was laid in perfect order. Wow. Look at that. What if she had taken that same skill and used that to make her money? The story tells us that she was aware of who these men were and the God they served. So, when the city officials came looking for them, it was apparent that she was also good at acting, because they believed her and went in another direction because of her statement.

Miki, what is the point that you're making?

Rahab was multi-talented. She was gifted in other areas that had absolutely nothing to do with sex. And, you are, too, my friend. A lot of women choose to fill voids that were created by a man, or in some cases, a woman, by having sex with multiple partners. Soul ties are created as a result of this promiscuous behavior, that are often hard to break when it's time for you to settle down. These soul ties remain attached and cause multiple personality disorders that prevent the proper functioning in life.

Right now, as you are reading this book, if for one second you have ever thought the only way you could be successful was to use your body, I want you to know that you are so much better than that. You have skills that may be hidden but can be revealed if you would adjust your focus, and beam in on who God created you to be. Don't let another person use your body for their dumping grounds!

Chapter Six

A Woman of Faith

The single most powerful woman on Earth, is a woman of prayer and great faith. Nothing moves God more than faith and it is literally impossible to please God without faith. Again, this doesn't mean you have to walk to the front of the church, become a saint, and live a religion bound lifestyle. It is necessary to realize you were created by a higher source for a higher purpose. Tapping into a spiritual connection and learning to remember who I was gave me the strength and supernatural power to break my curses and create a new way for myself even when it seemed like no way existed. Meditation led to prayer which opened a spirit connection. Find your spirituality immediately.

Show me a successful woman and I'll show you a woman with faith. I believe that the strength of this nation, our churches, and our families are built upon the foundation of a woman of faith. For women to be able to go through all that we go through, and be considered the weaker vessel, I must applaud us for not giving up and throwing in the towel.

Somehow, we bounce back from situations stronger, better, and more determined. Although we may cry, while we're crying, we keep moving. We find our motivation to keep pressing. We tap into this inner power that is connected to our faith and produce results that most any man would envy. Ladies, we are special.

I know, however, as we have discussed throughout the course of this book, there are days when your faith gets tired, and you don't want to believe anymore for anything. I know there are days when you don't want to be strong, you don't want to fight, and you wish that God would instantly answer your prayers versus making you wait. I am quite sure that there have been some nights when you laid awake trying to make yourself continue to believe what you have believed all your life. And that is, God is real, and He does hear you when you pray. Sometimes it can take God so long to answer and come through, that we struggle to keep believing that He even exists. Then there are other times where it seems God is solely focusing on making sure everything goes our way. There is a season for everything/

Brokenness is a process that has no set expiration time associated with it. It tests your faith and endurance and sometimes forces you to question if God is even real. Brokenness is a process that we go through and it can take some time for us to understand why but trust and believe there is a purpose for it. Am I saying it is necessary? Yes. How can pain be necessary? Pain is often the prerequisite to the promise. I am sure you have heard the analogy used somewhere before of a woman giving birth. Her pain of labor is necessary for her to birth her baby. Some things make no sense, but when you finally can see what God was working on, you will understand why you had to go through what you went through.

If you make it a habit to read the success stories of others, as I do, you will discover that anyone who was used by God in a major way was what we could consider broken at some point. They may be individuals who we all look up to now, but they will attest that they were greatly tested and broken in their spirit, but they used that as fuel to escape and lead powerful lives. However, in reading about these people who obviously had and have great faith, I have concluded that sometimes you must stop through the land of brokenness to get the lessons needed to help others who, too, must face broken times. After all, our purpose in life, and the trials and tribulations we go through, are not for us, but for the benefit, and blessing of other people. In my 30 years on earth I have overcome many trials, I am grateful now because all those circumstances showed how blessed I am that God still found me worthy and that so many other people need hope and encouragement.

Being broken is sometimes the best thing that can happen to you. You may have started this book thinking you were the worst person ever, having experienced the worst thing ever. But I hope by now you have received some inspiration that will result in you taking your broken pieces and making something great with them.

Something new.

Something more beautiful than what you had before. Because although broken, broken pieces still have value. No, seriously. I need you to know you are extremely valuable. You are worth more than millions, even billions. You are priceless. Everything you have been through up until this moment has been for a purpose—a cause. A purpose so great that even your imagination fails to comprehend. A purpose so great that it fails to compare to all you have had to go through to get to it.

If you are locked in what seems like a never-ending trial, just remember its part of your process. At some point, you're going to come out of the fire. Did you know that a refiner of silver always must keep his eye on the silver to not burn it? If kept one second longer than it's supposed to be in the fire, it'll burn. So, the silversmith has to watch it, and he knows it's ready when he can look over at the silver and see his reflection. My God! Don't you know that if a silversmith takes that much care with silver, your Heavenly Father is sure to take even better care of you. When He looks at you and can see His reflection, then He will take you out, and present you for all the world to see. All you must do is ask! I wanted to close this chapter out with an excerpt from one of my favorite teachers Joel Osteen's sermons which can be watched online if you search YouTube for "Bold Prayers- Joel Osteen". He says, "My question is, how wide is your mouth open? What are you asking for? Are you praying bold prayers, or are you praying get by prayers? However wide your mouth is open, that's what God is going to fill. And if you have a small vision, that's going to limit what God can do. It's not up to God, he has all power. It's up to you. And if you'll open your mouth wider and start praying bolder prayers, asking God to bring your dreams to pass, then you'll see God's goodness in a new way. God doesn't want you to go through life lonely, not fulfilled, never accomplishing your dreams. And when you ask boldly, you're not being selfish, you're not being greedy. You're releasing your faith. You're saying, "God, I believe you're the all-powerful Creator of the universe, and nothing is too hard for you". It's not enough to just think about it, it's not enough to just hope for it. Something supernatural happens when you ask. It puts a demand on your faith. When you're asked, God releases favor. When you ask, the angels go to work. When you ask, supernatural doors will begin to open.

Friends, when you pray bold prayers, you never know where God's going to take you. When you ask big, God will open supernatural doors. He'll connect you to the right people. God will go before you and make crooked places straight. He can even speak to you in dreams. What you couldn't make happen on your own, God can make happen for you. God controls the whole universe. He's not limited by your background, by what country you come from, by your education, by your talent. The only thing that limits God is our thinking.

Some of you are asking too small. God has placed seeds of greatness on the inside. He wants you to leave your mark on this generation. You're not supposed to live and die, and nobody miss you. Break out of your box. Start asking God for the hidden dreams he's placed on the inside.

See, when you pray God doesn't say, "Make sure it's practical. Make sure it's logical. Make sure it's reasonable. Make sure you can figure it out". No, he simply says, "Believe. Stay in faith". That's what allows God to do amazing things. If you will pray these bold prayers, you're going to see God show up and make a way when it looks like there is no way. You're going to see the surpassing greatness of God's favor. You're going to see a double portion. You're going to accomplish more than you thought possible. I believe and declare you will fulfill your God-given destiny. This is going to be an amazing year of faith, favor and victory for you. In Jesus' name."

Chapter Seven

The Strategy of Winning

So, you've gotten to the part of the book that's more informational. This is the work you must to outside of prayer for your Life Swap to happen. I can inspire you all day long, but if I don't teach you something, then I've not done my job in truly uplifting you.

Let me say this first. On the surface, the industry was great to me but, underneath it had been very damaging and tremendously unhealthy. I'm sure what comes to mind for most people are the horror stories of sex trafficking and forcible drug-induced sex brought on by pimps. But that wasn't my experience. Not even close. Outside of one bad "manager" who was upset because I chose to leave him, I lived a life of luxury, and were it not for the birth of my daughter, I don't know that I would've gotten out when I did. Matter fact, even when I made the decision to get out, I went back for a short period of time. I have never lied or shielded away from the truth about the process it takes to come out of this lifestyle, especially since I seemed to be empowered by it.

When I got out, I moved to Atlanta. What I found out when I left the life, was that I had no idea who I was outside the industry. I was clueless as to how life outside of my role as a professional companion worked. I was used to getting paid to make men feel happy, complete, and powerful. Mostly, very wealthy older men who had achieved everything in life but self-satisfaction. Although I was financially stable, emotionally I was certainly not. I began to discover that I was very disconnected from how to earn a real living outside of my looks, body, and charm. Talking to people became a burden because how could I build new relationships when I couldn't be honest about my past.

My fiancé and some other close friends helped me by introducing me to network marketing, and some other business opportunities that allowed me to fully retire from the lifestyle and build a new network. Once I had removed the facade of my alter ego, I had no idea who the person underneath was. I felt naked for the first time in my life. I went into the industry broken and unhealed from childhood trauma, and had recently went through a divorce with a husband that died two months later, and a horrible miscarriage with a man I thought I loved—and risked everything for—only to discover he was a serial cheater, and I simply was too weak to leave him. I hid all my pain in an alter ego of this beautiful, well put together woman, that demanded attention and admiration of men in high places. I didn't know how to be confident within myself minus the designer clothes, lavish trips, the glamour, the gifts and above all – the enormous amounts of attention that fueled my power. I began to look for labels to define myself. I poured myself into self-empowerment books, much like this one, and decided that I was going to win at life—but in a different way. I decided that I would forgive myself and I would not let my journey go in vain and settle for a mediocre life that most who leave the industry do. NO! I was going to get everything I believed I deserved. I would love God and stay close to Him. I would love myself and know that my body was worth more than money. I would allow myself to love a man completely for his heart and soul and allow that man to love me back. I would be a great and present mother who made sure my daughter knew her worth and was raised in a healthy environment. I would still be successful in a career that was not based on my body, but rather my gifts and talents. Above all, I would answer the call on my life to empower women and help them remember who they were and who they belonged to.

It's surprising how many people think everyone in the adult industry either walks the streets or are addicted to drugs. That's not the case. I have always been attracted to knowledge. Matter fact, I can contribute a lot of what I know to some of the regular clients I had who took the time to get to know me beyond the girlfriend experience. Many of them mentored me on business, world travel, and negotiating power. But, because of that stereotype, many people shun away from educating sex workers and try to mute their voices, thinking they have nothing meaningful to say or that they shouldn't have a desire for something greater—better.

I was doing some reading on the art of winning and I realized that there really is a method to it. If winning were truly the only important thing there would be no problem with hurting other people, cheating, lying, or stealing to achieve your objective. As we've seen too often over the past several years, many politicians, chief executives, and athletes who have made a fetish out of winning at all costs and have lost their careers, their marriages, their reputations, and sometimes even their freedom.

There is nothing intrinsically wrong with the idea of winning, but if we ignore the ethical responsibilities of avoiding harm, being honest, and treating others fairly, we will forfeit the most important thing of all: our own integrity. We often tell ourselves, "Where there's a will, there's a way." Think about how surprised you were the last time you accomplished something you thought would be too difficult to achieve. To the contrary, we also learn by losing, if we have the courage to pay attention. The best way to succeed the next time we attempt to do something, or to learn how to handle defeat better, is to find the lesson from our loss and take it to heart. If I had allowed what I labeled as my past failures to dictate my future, my future wins wouldn't have existed. I had no way of knowing that I would be a super successful entrepreneur a few years after leaving the life.

One thing you can't do on your journey to winning is berate yourself for losing. It isn't a decent way to treat yourself and doing so prevents you from getting back into action, which can lead to further losses. How many successful people do you know who are burdened by the weight of their past failures? I know I'm not. If you let losing get the best of you, it will be all but impossible to go forward. Allow yourself to feel what you feel, but accept reality, learn from the experience, don't be too hard on yourself, and move on. These guidelines are intended to help you make the best of a losing situation.

There is a great lesson to be learned from the book, "Rich Dad, Poor Dad" by Robert Kiyosaki. It is this: Set goals that are so easy to achieve, it takes no effort at all. Though "Rich Dad, Poor Dad" is a book primarily about money, Kiyosaki was referring to exercising — you know, the Going-to-the-Gym kind — when he talked about that. Don't set some ambitious goals. Just set your sight on something that's easy, effortless, that it's impossible for you to not achieve it. That's how you can build up the "habit" of winning. So, for example. Don't tell yourself you're going to leave the lifestyle cold turkey. Start with seeing less clients. Maybe one or two less. Get accustomed to the change you'll experience with doing that and then take the number up to maybe four or five. Of course, you'll see a dip on your finances, but use that as motivation to start your own business to supplement the income you're losing.

I am an ambitious person, and I set ambitious goals. Sometimes I achieve them, other times I don't. Even with me leaving the lifestyle, part of the strain was me stretching myself to meet the high standards I set for myself. The times when I failed, I'd beat myself up about it. What a stressful way to live. And it was all self-inflicted wounds. Kiyosaki's example in the book was about exercising. Let's say you set a goal to jog three miles every day. Well, I don't know how long it takes you to jog three miles, especially when you have never routinely run before. Maybe an hour? More? Scheduling that time every day is commitment. More power to you, if you can do it. I'm not saying you shouldn't do it — for some of us, we absolutely must face the stress and fear of failure to get up and do something. But for others, why not set more simplistic goals? How about one that is so easy to achieve that it takes no effort at all? Like putting your running shoes on.

So, adjust your goal to changing and putting your running shoes on. Everyday. How easy is that? If you did nothing else, you still accomplished your goal. You are a winner. You can check off that item for the day. Though, it's a shame to put shoes on for nothing. Surely, you can allow yourself to take a walk around the block. But no need to get more ambitious. In fact, my suggestion is not to do much more at the beginning. The important thing is to win more often.

I'm sure all of us feel positive about crossing off an item from our to-do list. Even the smallest victories add to your confidence and momentum. It gets you going. Now you have more excitement to go check something else off. It builds and enables you to accomplish goals that seemed unimaginable before. If your goal is to save money, put away a quarter, or a dollar, a day. Allow yourself to do more, if you can, but don't put pressure on yourself. I feel so much more comfortable in my own skin now that I win constantly, and don't live with the fear of failure as much.

The first place the enemy attacks is the mind. He knows that if he gets into our mind it will control our actions. I would like for you to take a moment to ask yourself a self-examining question. "What am I capable of?" "If the self-defeating attacks of my mind didn't exist, what could I achieve?" The answers to these questions open doors of opportunities we may have never thought possible. It's so common to see celebrities as "different." In our mind's eye, we place them in a different arena and then construct an arena for ourselves called "Not Good Enough" or "Could Never Do That." We so easily justify our lack of performance and minimize our potential for greatness. You must become aware of the array of thoughts that push you to quit. Let me break it to you. Even after a win, negative thoughts will come, but you must remain focused on achieving greatness.

So, yes, you can expect to have battles of the mind. The question is, what are you going to do about them? If you're not a positive thinker, if you don't have a positive attitude, you're in trouble. Without this quality or passion, everything becomes a "have to" instead of a "get to." For example, the woman who doesn't have a positive attitude says such things as: "I have to go to work today. I must clean the house. By contrast, a person of passion says, "I get to go to work today," because she knows that work is so much better than not having any work.

A woman of passion says, "I get to clean my house," because she is thankful to have a place to live. The truth is, if you're not a positive thinker, if you don't have a positive attitude, NOTHING can make up for it. Education can't. According to historians, some of America's worst presidents were supposedly the smartest and best educated. And some of the greatest Presidents, such as Abraham Lincoln, had very little formal education. A resume may get you through the door, but that's as far as it will get you. Talent can't. The world is filled with talented people who never achieve personal or professional success. Opportunity can't. An opportunity may open a door for you, but without positive thinking you won't make the most of your opportunity. In fact, it may never come to life. As professor Howard Hendricks said, "You don't put live eggs under dead chickens." But that's exactly what negative thinkers do. Other people can't. It is very difficult to be successful without the help of other people ... or at least be surrounded by the right kind of people. But even that won't guarantee your success because a team with no heart, no attitude, and no passion will not go very far.

There simply is no substitute for a positive attitude. It keeps you going when others quit. It releases an energy—an energy you don't even know you have and gets you through tough times. A positive attitude is the difference maker.

You, or someone you may know may have lost interest in life. Not much if anything turns you on anymore. Every day is just another day and another dollar. You've grown past the enthusiasms of your youth. You've decided that you're too old, or your life is too dismal, to maintain a positive attitude. But chances are, once again, you're doing very little to stimulate your attitude. Your attitude acts very much like a muscle. If you don't stimulate or exercise a muscle, it weakens. It deteriorates and eventually dies. And the same goes for your attitude. If you don't stimulate it, it dries up.

Keep on learning about the world, the people, and things outside of yourself. Get in the habit of looking forward to each day, wondering what new adventure will come your way. Learn to tie your attitude to a deeply held commitment rather than a passing emotion.

As I was reading, I read about one clergyman who had to learn this. He wrestled with how he could stand in front of his congregation and speak about peace, joy, love, hope, and faith when he didn't feel very enthusiastic at the moment he was speaking about those things. He didn't feel authentic. And yet he realized, if he yielded to his immediate feelings, if he let his sagging emotions influence his professional conduct, he could not inspire or motivate the people he was called to serve. The clergyman resolved his supposed "contradiction" by making an authentic choice. He chose to adhere to his calling rather than his personal emotions. He tied his attitude to something bigger and more important than his momentary feelings. You need to do the same thing no matter what line of work you may be in. To get and keep a positive attitude, tie your attitude to a long-term value. If you're in sales, tie your positive attitude to the quality of your product and the way it helps your customers. If you're in leadership, tie your positive attitude to your belief in growing people. Tie your attitude to doing what is right and good, no matter what job you have. That way you can "act" genuinely enthusiastic and "be" thoroughly positive no matter what you're feeling.

Getting and keeping a positive attitude is a not a once-and-for all proposition. It takes daily practice but fortunately less and less practice as you master these skills. Nonetheless, you still need to deal with the negative thoughts that come into your mind. Cancel them out. As one Doctor taught, "Whenever a negative thought about yourself and your abilities comes to mind, immediately cancel it out as unworthy, untrue, and unrealistic. The more vigorously you cancel it out, the weaker it becomes, until it disappears altogether." Don't give your negative thoughts too much attention. And don't put yourself down as being too small or too weak. Replace your negative thoughts with positive ones and you'll start getting positive results.

There is an art to winning, my loves, and once discovered, even when you feel as though you've lost, you will know that you have indeed won.

Chapter Eight

Eradicate the Doubt

You can read as many books as you'd like, hire as many life coaches as you can afford, and even go see a therapist or licensed counselor; but it won't matter if you don't believe that you have the power to win. No number of testimonials can convince you of this. The bottom line, this book, and the other resources that are available for one to read and draw inspiration, can only achieve so much when competing with one's will and one's outlook on themselves.

We discussed in the last chapter the importance of having a positive attitude. Second to that, it is important to make sure that no matter what happens, you never lose your confidence to win. Once a person loses their confidence, their chances of winning lessens, and if the behavior is continued, the outlook will almost always end up in loss.

One of the biggest flaws growing up that followed us into our adulthood is our constant need to be accepted. Most of us do not understand, nor do we appreciate, our individuality. We constantly compare ourselves to others to the point that we lose sight of our own identity. I think it is safe to say that a significant amount of our broken pieces is a direct result of us trying to be someone we aren't. What am I saying? I am saying that we can be the generator for our brokenness.

Mary J. Blige wrote a song entitled, "Take Me As I Am," and the line goes on to say, "or have nothing at all." In other words, you can either like me, love me, or leave me. Boy, if I had that mentality growing up and even after I was an adult, I would have spared myself a whole lot of tears and heartache.

You were created to be unique.

Different.

When it comes to you, there should not be a "normal." But so many have gotten lost in the glaze of society's expectations until they no longer recognize their worth or value. So, as soon as someone says something negative about them, or speak negative to them, they crawl into the shadows broken by the words of another broken human being. How sad it would be for you to get to the end of your life and discover that you never lived? How sad would it be to get to the end of your life only to have people shake their head in disappointment that you allowed anybody, or anything, to stop you from being all you were designed to be. That would be sad, and it would be an atrocity.

Not long ago, I read somewhere that babies function at a genius level until the age of one. When you think about their mental and emotional growth in that first year, they learn that their ten fingers and toes are a part of them; they learn that when they cry, Mom picks them up; they learn that when Dad makes a funny face or touches them in a certain way, the sound of laughter comes out and makes them feel good; they somehow are able to decipher strange utterances into meaningful expression of language and no matter whether they fall ten times, one hundred times, or a thousand times, the thought of "it is too hard" or "I can't" never enters their tiny minds as they learn how to walk. However, as children get older, the ability to process and absorb a tremendous amount of sensory input slows down significantly, and by adulthood there are few among us who can truly be called geniuses. This raises an interesting question: If there is truth to this decline in cognitive function, what is the cause?

Research has suggested that the steady and rapid decline in this high level cognitive function is the learned behavior of self-doubt and self-judgement, often imposed on us by meaningful parents that have taught us, "You can't be a firefighter, it's too dangerous," "You can't be a doctor, you're not smart enough, you don't focus enough, and besides, medical school costs a lot of money," or "Honey, there is no money in being an artist, why don't you be a lawyer instead?" It is no wonder that our sense of wonder and our sense of invincibility has evaporated with the genius in us.

Self-doubt is one of the major obstacles to living the life you truly deserve. This unhealthy food for the soul drags down your spirit, crushes your ambitions, and prevents you from achieving all that you can. We all have those inner voices inside our heads that tell us we are not good enough, not strong enough and incapable of doing the things we dream of. Often, these feelings of weakness or incompetence stem from childhood and become ingrained in our very being. Over time, self-doubt can lead to problems with anxiety and depression, which in turn can lead to serious physical ailments like weight gain, high blood pressure, chronic fatigue and even increased mortality rates among those with heart disease. It is important not only to be aware of the destructive nature of these feelings, but to incorporate methods to counteract this negativity so that you can enjoy a joyful, productive and fulfilling life.

<u>Tips for Dealing With Self-Doubt</u>

-Live in the Present

Most of the time, feelings of self-doubt are attached to memories of times in the past when you failed to achieve something or when somebody else told you that you were not good enough. Don't dwell on those moments. Try to ground yourself and think about the now. Just because you couldn't accomplish something before doesn't mean you can't do it again. Every day is a new start and a new chance to go for what you really want.

-Trust in Yourself

Sometimes we can be our own worst enemies. If you tell yourself that you cannot do something, then you probably won't even try it in the first place. Have faith in yourself, tell yourself that you are just as capable as the next person of achieving your dreams, and stop listening to the voice inside that keeps saying, "I can't."

-Counteract the Negative

At times, it may seem as though the negative voices in your head are stronger than the positive voices. Try to be aware of this when it happens and make a concerted effort to counteract these negative thoughts with positive energy. When you feel a negative thought coming on, simply remind yourself about the things you like about yourself, your strengths, and all the things you have achieved in your life and are proud of.

-Find the Source of Your Self-Doubt

If you find yourself constantly telling yourself you are not good enough, you may want to delve into the root of the problem. Where did these feelings originate? Was there a specific event that has caused you to harbor such feelings? You can choose to do this on your own or with the help of a professional therapist. Once you identify and understand the source of the problem, you can begin to work toward eliminating those negative thought patterns.

-Spend Time With Others

Friends and family are an invaluable source of strength, assurance, and encouragement. In fact, studies propose that people who have strong social support have fewer cardiovascular issues and lower levels of cortisol, otherwise known as the stress hormone, when compared to people with fewer friends. Even strangers can be positive and helpful when it comes to self-doubt. Simply voicing your self-doubt to others can often put it in perspective and make you realize how illogical this negativity can be. In addition, other people can offer advice and support that will motivate you and give you a huge confidence boost.

Wouldn't it be amazing if you could rediscover the genius in you with no regard to your past even if your past is littered with shameful behavior such as that of a sex worker? The simple act of believing in yourself, trusting the process, and trusting that you will know what to do when the time comes, can greatly relieve your self-doubt. Practice staying present in the moment and try not to regret the past or worry about the future. If you can do this, you may just see your genius reemerge.

Way too many people walk through life carrying the heavy weight of self-doubt. Deep down, they fear that they are missing some essential quality that would make them truly successful socially (worthy of love) or in other aspects of life. They worry about friends and loved ones leaving them; or thinking less of them because of something they've done or failed to do. They feel down on themselves, lacking the self-confidence and assertiveness to accomplish, or appreciate meeting, goals.

If either of these describe you, it's important to understand that you don't just feel this way. You actively maintain these painful experiences and self-perceptions through the ways that you think. Believe it or not, this is good news. It offers you a way to feel better about yourself by changing how you think and relate to yourself.

People who are insecure often only notice situations or feedback that confirms their lack of value. They often downplay their strengths –Oh, anyone could have painted that. And they barely notice other people's appreciation of them.

Think about it: Is this something you do? Consider the past week. Did you tend to pay attention to things that show you lack value or make you feel inadequate?

Choose to attend to more positive feedback about you: Choose to consciously listen for positive feedback. You will be inclined to minimize the

importance of it. For now, that's okay. The important step here is to recognize that it exists.

Another way that people keep themselves feeling unloved or inadequate is, they fail to remember evidence of them being worthwhile or successful people. They can't remember anything particularly good that they did, and don't remember any meaningful positive feedback – which is easy to do. When you believe you aren't truly capable or worthy of love, it's easy to interpret everything in that light. Your spouse is tired at the end of the day, so he/she must not really want to be with you. Your supervisor returned your report with suggestions for making changes; so, she must not be happy with your work. What you fail to recognize is that your way of making sense of these situations may be more about your insecurity than them not caring or thinking positively of your work.

People who have very low self-esteem are almost always ultra-critical of themselves, they have a raging inner critic and continually put themselves down, and even when they achieve something quite significant, they never reward themselves. They never allow themselves to digest or own or celebrate the good experiences that they generate and create in their lives. And not only do they not reward themselves, but they don't receive compliments easily either.

Self-value grows through true regard and respectful acknowledgement and recognition. Just think about the way children respond to positive feedback. Even if a child is encouraged build confidence, if achievement is never recognized and celebrated then the feel-good factor will be missing, and the outcome won't be internally consolidated.

Jesse Jackson had a famous speech back in the day that was dubbed, "Keep Hope Alive." If I may, I want to switch gears a little and talk about how to keep hope alive in your life when it appears self-doubt is choking the life out of you.

In this world, our hope is constantly under attack. So, it must be nourished and strengthened. Hope isn't automatic by any means; it doesn't just happen. On the contrary, it's something we must try to maintain. Otherwise, over time it will wither, it will diminish to the point that it can't support us; it will fail us when the trials come. Hope is something all human beings have in common, at least, that is, until circumstance after circumstance proves to be disappointing until hopelessness sets in. Hope is a feeling that carries with it the possibilities of things to come which are expected to happen. Without hope, mankind would cease to push forward, opening hearts and minds toward finding resolve for; "How can this be made better?" or "What is the next effective step?" or simply, "I desire...and because I desire it I [hope] to attract it."

Hope is a very positive, higher vibration feeling which leads to unconditional love. The reality is, hope is a feeling that everyone experiences for something. Even those who feel hopeless about their deepest desires or long sought-after goals have hope. It may be the feeling of getting better when in despair; or staying in bed when not wanting to get up; a cure for an illness just diagnosed; or to be loved enough to not be left alone; etc. So, when examining the prospects of experiencing hopelessness, never fear, hope does exist. It's a matter of discovering where hope lies and then keeping it alive through some very specific methods.

One way to keep hope alive is by maintaining faith. Faith is an action one takes based on the belief and hope of a goal being reached, a desire being realized or a known certainty for any type of outcome to happen. When faith is maintained a step is taken toward the desired goal which is hoped to be realized. And, if the next step and then the next steps are taken, hope is no longer required because the outcome has been reached. I liken this to the "faith" caterpillars have when they whirl and spin a cocoon encasing their bodies in the hope they will emerge from this self-made casket.

Think about it; the caterpillar dies in order to become reborn and anything could happen in the process. A predator could get to the cocoon; a human could pluck it from its resting place and destroy the cocoon; an animal could trample it or knock it off its perch. That caterpillar must trust and hope it makes it to the other side when in the chrysalis state. Yet, it creates, through faith, the cocoon anyway. And, for the cocoon which remains intact, the rebirth of a beautiful butterfly emerges where freedom of the realized desire is met. Without faith hope may as well be dead; because that would be the point where whatever the goal is, it is given up on. There is no proceeding forward and no need to have faith where action isn't required. So, faith is one of the most primary singularly significant aspects of keeping hope alive.

There is another measure, too, on how to keep hope alive. Faith is the number one and most important thing to do. Like all the manifesting aspects of living in this world, the universal laws work based on energetic as well as physical action, and faith incorporates both aspects. Therefore, it's so powerfully attached to maintaining hope. But the other way of keeping hope alive plays an important role in assisting the process of moving through despair. It is represented as physical action, through faith, but its power lies in the energetic realm where all manifestation begins. This is the power of personal development which offers an array of possibilities for the illuminating light of hope to be sustained.

When you stay focused on what you desire and the goal(s) to get there, hope is certainly being maintained. Every day you are telling yourself; "This is what I am creating as part of my experience," in a very conscious way. The best way to focus on your goals and desires is to write down very specifically what it is. Then make a point of looking at it and reading it out loud daily. If your mind is idle thinking about things that seem unimportant, think about your desire. After a while it will sink into your subconscious mind where you will always be focused on it without thinking about it. In this way, you will attract your desire along with the necessary circumstances to bring it about.

When going into battle, the wisest general learns to know his enemy very, very well. You can't defeat the enemy without knowing him. And when you're trying to overcome a negative self-image and replace it with self-confidence, your enemy is yourself. Get to know yourself well. Start listening to your thoughts. Start writing a journal about yourself, and about the thoughts you have about yourself, and analyzing why you have such negative thoughts. And then think about the good things about yourself, the things you can do well, the things you like. Start thinking about your limitations, and whether they're real limitations or just ones you've allowed to be placed there, artificially. Dig deep within yourself, and you'll come out (eventually) with even greater self-confidence.

It's hard to be confident in yourself if you don't think you'll do well at something. Beat that feeling by preparing yourself as much as possible. Think about taking an exam: if you haven't studied, you won't have much confidence in your abilities to do well on the exam. But if you studied your butt off, you're prepared, and you'll be much more confident. Now think of life as your exam and prepare yourself. You didn't come out of the womb unsure of your cry or insecure about your large umbilical cord. You came out completely unaware of external judgment, concerned only with your own experience and needs. I'm not suggesting you should be oblivious to other people. It's just that it may help to remember confidence was your original nature before time started chipping away at it. Once you developed a sense of self-awareness, you started forming doubts and insecurities about how other people saw you. You learned to crave praise and avoid criticism, and maybe you started getting down on yourself if you got more of the latter than the former.

When you start feeling unsure of yourself remember we were all born with confidence, and we can all get it back if we learn to silence the thoughts that threaten it. "Confidence comes not from knowing you know everything, but from knowing you can handle what comes up." — Don King

No one in the world knows everything. Everyone is good at some things and not so good at others. Don't weigh your security against what you know or can do; weigh it against your willingness and capacity to learn. If someone criticizes you, take it is an opportunity to improve. If someone does better than you, see it as an opportunity to learn from them. If you fall short at something, realize you can get closer next time. Don't worry if you're not confident in what you can do now—be confident in your potential.

Like anything else in life, your confidence will improve with practice. A great opportunity to do this is when you meet new people. Just like if you were the new kid in school, they have no idea who you are—meaning you have an opportunity to show them. As you shake their hand, introduce yourself, and listen to them speak, watch your internal monologue. If you start doubting yourself in your head, replace your thoughts with more confident ones. Ask yourself what a confident person would do and then try to emulate that. People are more apt to see you how you want to be seen if they suspect you see yourself that way.

Above all, remember you are capable and worthy—just as much as anyone else, regardless of what you've achieved, regardless of what mistakes you've made. Knowing that intellectually, is the first step to believing it in your heart. Believing it is the key to living it. And living it is the key to reaching your potential.

Chapter Nine
Don't Lose Focus

No matter what you set out to win at in life, it will only result in a win IF you remain focused. There are so many things that pop up in our lives daily that will assist in us being distracted, which ultimately causes us to forget what we were trying to do in the first place. I always tell people that distractions only come to get us to forfeit the real blessing that is almost always on the other side of it.

A distraction is an unhealthy attraction that breaks your focus and hinders you. It claims your attention from the valuable task at hand and consumes it on something of lesser value or importance at that time. Distractions are insidious by nature. They pull you away from your intentions, and the more we try to ignore them the more they lure us into an abyss of wasted time and potential. We get distracted primarily for two reasons, they protrude out of the ordinary or they provide us with some form of pleasure.

Psychologists calls this type of distraction bottom up thinking. This occurs when you try to focus on a task but something out of the ordinary happens that demands attention and overrides intention. It could be as extreme as a loud noise, or as subtle at a spot of blue on a red canvas. These external distractions fall into the pink elephant syndrome, no matter how hard you try to ignore it, it carries enough psychic weight

to draw your attention.

Internal distractions are much more sinister. They come from our subconscious mind and depending upon the root cause, they are often the tool of self-sabotage. Internal distractions bring us pleasure in the form of thoughts. These thoughts are generated from a host of reasons. It could be because you don't like the task at hand, you feel incompetent, you have emotional distress or euphoria in another area of life, etc. But here is the deviousness of internal distractions; the thoughts that occur to distract us may have little to no resemblance of the root cause for the distraction.

For example, while writing this book I have had several distracting thoughts that suggested maybe the timing isn't right to share this, or what if nobody subscribes to the message I'm trying to convey. After all, I have put it off other times before. It didn't matter how many times people said, "Michaela, when are you going to write a book," I still found reasons to not do it. Reasons and excuses are two different things, but that's a whole other book. The bottom line and the fact remain, I allowed things to distract me from completing the book you are reading now. It took me applying to my own life what you are reading, before I made up my mind that I would lose the distractions so I could win at this accomplishment that has been a long time coming.

The best way to handle distractions is to acknowledge them and not try to ignore them. When you try to censor attention getters, you empower them to get more attention. Besides, distractions become craftier when we try to "un-think" the thought, "un-see" the sight, or "un-hear" the sound. But you must acknowledge a distraction for what it is – a distraction. The only reason a distraction is so effective is because they work subconsciously, but when I know I am distracted then I can return to my intentions quicker. To acknowledge the distraction, you can follow the biblical

guidelines that tell us to take every thought captive (2 Corinthians 5:5). We take the thought captive by addressing our internal dialogue. The best way to address an internal dialogue is to bring the conversation out of your head so that your words can control it. You can practice just by repeating, "This _____ will not distract me. I am going to win at this."

Another thing you must do is deal with distractions immediately. If a distracting thought was important enough to get your attention deal with it immediately. Don't ignore it and hope that it will not resurface later, because when it does it will probably come up at the most inopportune time. Besides, dealing with it now is a much more effectual use of your time and mental energy than having to ignore it again the next time it distracts you. So, if your mind reminds you of an important task while you're in the middle of something else, write it down or decide not to do it, but don't ignore it. Deciding not to do something is not the same as not deciding to do something.

I ran across something called time boxing which is a time management technique used to stay focused and maximizes the productivity of free or little time. There are many different variations of it, but the way it works best for me is when I set a certain amount of time to do a task and I set a reward at the end of that task. For example, as I was writing this book, I will complete a chapter and then reward myself with a good ol' talk-about-nothing conversation with one of my girlfriends to allow my mind to rest. My focus wasn't to finish the book, but to finish a chapter. When I do this, I find I break apathy and create a focus that minimizes internal distractions. It is also a great way to overcome procrastination.

Often internal distractions are the symptoms of deeper issues on the inside. Having the ability to recognize and deal with those issues will go a long way in helping you to stay focused and productive. Often emotions are the biggest culprit, so in order to get to the root cause you must identify the cause of the emotion. For example, lack of confidence could generate fear or lethargy while disdain for a task could generate frustration, irritation, and even anger. The distractors from these issues could be anything from daydreaming about your next vacation to wondering why you didn't get the Louboutins. The key is to read these emotions like signpost that would lead you to a cause. Once the cause is identified and well defined you become empowered to overcome the issue and the distractions that they cause.

Have you heard this saying? The most important thing is to remember the most important thing. What are the most important things to you? In your life as a whole? During an interaction with someone? Right this minute?

The most important things often get pushed to the sidelines. Modern life is full of distracting clamor, from text messages and emails, to window displays in the mall. Other people tug at you with their priorities - which may not be your own. And it can feel scary to admit what really matters to you and go after it for real, for real. Not to mention the voices that whisper in the back of the mind: What if you fail?

1. Establish daily rituals. You can't truly tend to your goals if you keep putting them off. It's easy to fall into the habit of saying, "Tomorrow. I'll get to that tomorrow." Yet, tomorrow is the today you were putting off

yesterday. Try to work on your goals daily, even if only in the slightest ways.

2. Set realistic goals. I know I've mentioned this before, but it's worth repeating. It's difficult to stay focused if you're goals are highly unrealistic. Chances are, you aren't going to the moon. But hey, that's okay. It's more fulfilling for your spirit and ego to set goals you can accomplish. Don't make them too easy but be sure you have realistic ambitions in mind.

3. Visualize your goals. Are you trying to lose weight? Visualize your slimmer body in a bikini. Have you been saving up for a new car? Imagine yourself driving it, breathing in that new car smell. The point is, visualizing your goals fuels your need to reach them, which only keeps your focus on your end goal.

4. Give yourself "me" time. It is 100% healthy to take mental breaks from time to time. You do need to give yourself some time to wind down and relax. None of us are superwoman (or man), so it's natural to need a break from high levels of goal keeping. Take these brief breaks to do the things you love.

5. Be focused on staying focused. Remind yourself to concentrate on your goals. Maintaining focus is a skill all of us need to remember, as it's easy to get distracted. However, if you keep your goals at the front of your mind and remember to give them careful attention, you will likely keep your focus strong, and your eyes on the prize!

Friends, I need you to understand, and accept, that because you were created with purpose there will be many things ALWAYS coming at you. You will never be void of temptations or distractions. As the saying goes, you are what you eat; well in this case, you are what you think.

"I don't have the education for that."

"I'm not good enough."

"I'm not worthy."

"I'll never achieve that."

"I know God is able, but maybe it's just not for me."

"That will NEVER happen for me."

Have you ever caught yourself thinking those thoughts, or saying those words verbally? If so, let me be the one to tell you those are all lies. Whatever you accept as your truth becomes your reality. God lets us know that whatever a man thinks in his heart is the kind of man he is. Take a quick moment and do a life inventory. Some of the things that have gone wrong in your life may be some of the very things you have declared out of your own mouth without realizing the damage you were causing to yourself. We constantly say how broke we are, and then wonder why our finances never improve. We constantly say how we will never be happy, and then complain about never being happy. For those that are single, you keep saying you will never find the right mate, and then wonder why the right mate never comes along. The more you repeat negative words, the more negativity becomes true in YOUR life, but the good news is it doesn't have to remain YOUR truth.

"Whether you think you can, or you think you can't – you're right." ~Henry Ford

The above quote holds a lot of truth. In other words, however you perceive a situation, is what that situation will be. If you are the kind of person who always pulls out the 'bad' about a situation, then 'bad' will always be your outcome. Is your glass half full or half empty? Just think, it's the same glass, and both concepts mean the same thing, but there's a positive meaning as well as a negative one. It's all in how you view it. The beautiful thing about GOD is that he's a loving GOD. He loves you and He want to adjust your thinking so it can line up with His plans for your life. The same way you became negative through your thoughts, you can also become a positive using the same method and technique. Yes, it's easy to doubt God and yourself. Especially when your inner voice is telling you that you're not going to make it. When your inner voice is telling you that you're all washed up. When your inner voice is telling you that just because you haven't always valued your body, you won't find a man who will. When your inner voice is telling you that you will always have to depend on someone paying you for sexual services in order to make ends meet. When your inner voice is telling you that you're going to sink. When your inner voice is telling you that you're not worth saving. When the waves are washing over in your life's ship. It's easy to look at the circumstances around you. But God is the God of your circumstances. He is the God of your impossibilities!

So, don't be distracted by the waves of life.

Don't be distracted by the losses of life.

Don't even be distracted by the failures.

Because if you can just keep your focus and keep believing; God will complete the work that He began in you!

Chapter Ten

Life Swap

I know, I know. You've gone through so much, and have lost so much you don't think it's possible to win, right? At least five of you reading this book have given up on the possibility that winning is even attainable because disappointment has purchased a permanent space in your life. But I came to deliver an eviction notice to that mindset and disenchantment.

It.

Has.

To.

Go.

Now.

Even after one gets over a failure or disappointment, there are some that leave scars that serve as reminders of the permanent damage left behind.

Imagine the current lives of the parents of the many teenagers who have been gunned downed on the cold, violent streets of Chicago; or the divorce that took place between a couple who had been married for twenty years; or the family who lost their home to foreclosure and are struggling to find shelter for their children; or the child who lost both their parents in a car accident and are forced to live from one foster care home to another; or the elderly man or woman whose body is stricken with cancer. When those type things happen, you never forget them. You may learn to live through them, but they change you forever. I am certain if you look on your body there are scars that are still there that remind you of a fall you took as a child. While the pain is no longer felt, the scar is there—forever. Even when bones are broken, they may heal, but it is not uncommon to feel an ache or pain ten years later. Beloved, what I am saying to you is, some disappointments come specifically to break you. The enemy is not concerned with you just getting an injury and having to sit out of a game, he is aiming to break you enough to put you OUT of the game. His goal is to get you so broken and discouraged until you have no strength to persevere. You've read and heard that the race is not given to the swift or the strong, but to the one who endures to the end. He is not after your start; he is after your finish.

Some of the worst breaking points come after some of your best victories. Ever have a season where it seems everything was going the way you wanted it to go and no sooner than you can get comfortable, shit hits the fan? Imagine getting a job promotion on Friday and then walk into your office on Monday and suddenly, the entire staff has decided to become your newfound enemies, consequently making your job difficult to do or tolerate. Imagine a couple celebrating their wedding anniversary on Saturday and then on Monday morning instead of having breakfast together, they are in their attorney's office filing for divorce. How can that be?

Displeasure's goal is to get you to give up just before you cross the finish line. One of the enemy's best tactics of doing this is to keep moving the finish line so you fail to see that you're making progress. This is meant to tire you out because he knows that if you ever get the resilience you need to persevere, you will be a force to reckon with. There are a lot of people who could do great and wonderful things in life, but we will never know who they are for many of them have taken a seat on the sidelines of life. Can you imagine watching a football or basketball game and all the star players were on the bench? Of course not. I wish I could sit from the seat of God and look at the many people across the world who are operating lower than their potential because they've grown weary.

My dearest friends, can I encourage you with one of my favorite Bible verses? Galatians 6:9 says, "And let us not be weary in well doing: for in due season we shall reap, if we faint not." The first thing I want you to know is you are doing well. I know things have been hard. I know the road has been tough, but considering all you've been through, you have done well. The fact that you are still in your right mind and not sitting in the corner of a room the size of a prison cell waiting for medication, is a testament of just how well you've done. The fact that you were able to forgive those who hurt you and pray for them during them doing you wrong is a testament that you've done well. The fact that you find a way to get out of your bed, go to work, care for your family, and live a decent life is a testament that you've done well. Some of you know you were supposed to have lost it by now, but God has kept you in perfect peace. No, you may not have made all the right decisions. You may not have stayed on course, but you kept going, and that is enough for me to say, you've done well. I, for one, am proud of you.

A lot of people give up right before we enter our appointed season. How many times do we forfeit our blessings because we give up? How many blessings go unclaimed because we throw in the towel?

Here's what I want you to do. I want you to tap into your inner spirit and speak what's true. And what's true? I'm glad you asked. For starters, you are victorious. You are more than a conqueror. As a matter of fact, you need to confess that daily. Do not allow anyone to tell you who you are. Do not allow anyone to suppress and stifle you another day. You are closer to victory than you realize. Get up, wash your face, and press your way.

Ladies, it's time you let go of the hurt of the past. Do something for yourself. Go and get your hair done again. If you can't grow it, weave it. Get you some make-up, put on your heels, and strut with the confidence that you are a winner. More importantly, you are the epitome of an over comer. That last loss really did come to take you out, but, my God, you are still here. You survived!

Stop feeling like a failure. Things may not have turned out like you wanted it to. You may not be financially where you thought you would be by now, but it really is alright. You still have time. Take what you have and make it work. Stop walking around with your head held down. You have no reason at all to be ashamed any longer. Your past does not dictate your future. The only failure in life is failing to try again.

I pray this chapter will reignite something within you, my sister, to get up and give life a try one more time. Why? Because you win in the end! I believe there is a little something left in you that desires to be excellent and great, but you are afraid. Afraid of disappointment. Afraid to be hurt again. Afraid that it may not work. But, within you is the power of resurrection.

You can get up.

You can start over.

You can try again.

There is a story often told of a woman who suffered a blood disease for twelve years. It is recorded that she spent all her money going from one doctor to the next, so to the point it practically bankrupts her. But, even after twelve years, no health insurance, enduring castigation from the community; when Jesus comes through her town holding a crusade, she finds the strength to get up, get dressed, and make her way to him. She had no idea if He could help her or if she would even get to Him, but she tried anyway. She left home not knowing what she would encounter. She left home not knowing if she would be stopped.

As she made her way, she had to press through the other people who were falling at his feet. She had to make her way past the people who were surrounding Him seeking their own miracles. She did not care where He was on His way to; she just knew that she needed a miracle. And her need for a miracle was greater than any desire she may have had to stay in her place of desperation. I am sure the voices in her head mocked her as she got dressed. Mocked her as she walked out of the door and saw the swarm of people trying to get his attention. But, despite it all, we all know she got her healing after having touched the hem of the master's garment. How desperate are you to make it to YOUR miracle?

How driven are you to get what God has promised you? How determined are you to keep going to see what the end is going to bring? I was so desperate that I gave up everything that I knew and had grown to be comfortable in. I left my toxic relationship, left the high paying immoral lifestyle, left the rewinding destruction of mentally replaying my past, left the state where life was easy, left my family, and left my way of thinking. I gave it all to God in exchange for His mercy, forgiveness, favor, and love. It was the best decision I have ever made.

The most persistent person will usually win. There are plenty of talented, highly intelligent, and educated people out there. Why aren't they all successful? Not to keep beating a dead horse, but my guess would be their mindset. Perhaps they don't believe they can achieve what they want or set their sights low to avoid the risk of failure and pain. We can learn a lot from people like Henry Ford—a man of average intelligence who surrounded himself with the very best people. His job was to consider their input and make decisions accordingly. So, even if you don't currently have the know-how, or whatever you think is holding you back to achieve your dream right now, know that you will eventually if you continue to make proactive efforts towards your goal. It's just a matter of time.

The sharpest individuals are continually learning from whatever source presents itself. This means getting expert knowledge in their field and learning how to do things in general. But it also means listening along the way for ideas that you can implement directly in new or current projects. Here is the point: It doesn't matter who the ideas come from. Constantly look outside yourself for new ideas and be flexible. This also helps with ensuring a victory. Your results are also a source of learning if you'll listen to them. This applies to both successes and failures. If you succeed at something, it's not because you're invincible-it's because you took certain actions that produced a certain result. Same goes for failures. Focus more on actions and results and what they can teach you through trial and error, rather than making things personal.

I wanted to write this book because I wanted people like you, the ones people turn their nose up at because of what you do or have done for a living, to know that you can win. Yes, sometimes you must lose people and things in order to win. My strained relationship with my family was a loss. Losing friends who I thought had my best interest at heart was a loss. Allowing myself to be used for a man's pleasure when deep down I wanted just one man who I could give my all to in a relationship—a loss. But you're reading this book right now because I took all those losses and STILL declared victory. I took all that hurt and disappointment and channeled it into something great. A movement. A force that can't be stopped. I could have continued to harbor and swim in my failures, but I chose to be better. Do better. And, the same way I discovered the power to do it, so can you. You do not have to let a loss prohibit you from your next victory.

I cannot promise you will not face anymore trials.

I wish I could tell you that you've jumped your last hurdle. But, I cannot.

I wish I could tell you that you've experienced your final loss. I cannot promise you've cried your last tear.

But here is what I can tell you.

I can tell you your latter will be greater than your former.

I can tell you your best days are ahead of you.

I can tell you God is going to restore to you what the enemy thought he got away with.

So, don't you dare give up, don't you dare give in. You have come too far to give up now!

For the race is not given to the swift, nor the battle to the strong, but it is given to the one who endures until the end! Remember SWAP means to start with a prayer. When you submit to Gods will and allow him to use you as a vessel to complete his plan you can experience a life you never dreamed possible. Be bold in your prayers and have faith that there is no request that God cannot grant.

Conclusion

(An excerpt from Code Living)

In our society being a winner is what symbolizes success. Victory is the ultimate factor and we live and die by it. We don't tolerate failure and it isn't an option. If somebody fails in our society, he or she is demeaned as unsuccessful.

But "don't panic" I am only mentioning extremes. Most people fall somewhere in the grey area (closer to the winning side) between winning and losing. The public is generally successful at something's but then lose at others. They are successful enough to be recognized but then don't fail enough to be forgotten.

To give you a better idea of this scale, an example of person who is failing at life could be a homeless person, who while having the resources around stays homeless.

1. Winners Are Driven

Winners are very ambitious and driven about what they want to achieve. They don't take no for answer and self-motivate themselves to keep going. *"I've missed more than 9000 shots in my career. I've lost almost 300 games. 26 times, I've been trusted to take the game winning shot and missed. I've failed over and over and over again in my life. And that is why I succeed."* – Michael Jordan

2. Winners Take Responsibility

Winners hold themselves accountable for what happens in their lives and don't blame external factors. They feel they are in control of their destiny and don't let others decide that for them.

3. Winners Are Eager to Learn

Winners are always learning and are always looking for new ways to challenge themselves. They never feel like they know enough, and they truly understand that knowledge really is power.

4. Winners Are Positive Thinkers

Winners always take an optimistic perspective towards life and are always trying to leverage the field in their favor.

Watch your thoughts, they become words.

Watch your words, they become actions.

Watch your actions, they become habits.

Watch your habits, they become character.

Watch your character, for it becomes your destiny.

5. Winners Are Humble

Winners never let their ego get in the way of their success. They know what's more important. And don't keep a short-term mentality. While they are modest on the inside, they know their worth and are confident in their abilities.

6. Winners Are Certain

Winners don't doubt their actions or decisions. They focus on what they are going to do next and "Pull the Trigger". They don't overthink negative thoughts and stand by their actions.

7. Winners Set Goals

Winners are very goal oriented. They decide on what they want and when they want it.

And then do whatever they morally can to reach it.

"Discipline is the bridge between goals and accomplishment."– Jim Rohn

8. Winners Focus on Solutions

Rather than focusing on the problem, winners focus on how to solve the problem. They don't let the past hang over them and work on solutions.

9. Winners Work Hard

Winners put in their best effort and never run away from work. They have a relentless engine and they keep pushing forward no matter what the face. They are driven and yearn for success.

10. Winners Act

Winners never refrain from action and are always the first to start. They don't need a reminder to begin working and become legendary.

11. Winners Listen

Winners pay attention to others and think before they speak. They know that don't have all the answers and know that they need the help of others to reach their goals. *"Most people do not listen with the intent to understand; they listen with the intent to reply."* – Stephen R. Covey

12. Winners Are Passionate

Winners love what they do and are passionate about life. They use this inner obsession to fuel them and push them forward; especially when the going gets tough.

13. Winners Are Willing to Stand Alone

Winners are very independent, and they understand that the path to victory is sometimes a lonely one. While they are great at communication and networking, they are the best lone wolfs.

14. Winners are Self-Motivators

Winners can motivate themselves when it gets tough and are able to keep going. They have a permanent fire inside of them that always burns for success.

15. Winners Constantly Expand Their Comfort Zone

Winners constantly explore challenges and opportunities to expand their comfort zone. They know that being satisfied means you're not improving and always try to stay on edge.

16. Winners Have Strong Will Power

Winners can withstand all kinds of hurdles and hardships. They have good self-discipline and can control their mind and body. Their body is their temple.

17. Winners Have High Self-Esteem

Winners know what they are worth, and they feel good about themselves. They are self-assured and don't need external approval to keep them steady.

18. Winners Are Persistent

Winners do whatever it morally takes to achieve their goals. They don't easily give up and don't let small obstacles get in their way. They push and push and keep pushing until they reach their goal.

19. Winners Aren't Afraid of Failure

Winners know that to reach success they will have to at one time or another face failure. So rather than being afraid of failure, they embrace it and learn form. Winners use failure to motivate themselves even further. *"Failure should be our teacher, not our undertaker. Failure is delay, not defeat. It is a temporary detour, not a dead end. Failure is something we can avoid only by saying nothing, doing nothing, and being nothing."* – Denis Waitley

20. Winners Don't Procrastinate

Winners don't put things off and try to get things done as soon as possible. They understand the value of time and try to make every second time.

21. Winners Are Focused

Winners are always dedicated and focused towards whatever they are doing. They know that multi-tasking is a myth and they try to be as productive as possible.

22. Winners Try to Find A Better Way

Winners experiment and don't put all their eggs in one basket. They know they are always better ways of doing things. And they try to find what they are.

23. Winners Are Alert

Winners are both physical and mentally alert. They are always on the lookout for changes in their surroundings. They don't sit idly like vegetables and are always ready to act.

24. Winners Are Confident

Winners believe in themselves, their abilities and their talents. They are conformable in their own skin and embrace their strengths and weaknesses.

25. Winners Manage Their Time

Winners are very productive and know how to spend their time wisely. They know that life is limited and that ever moment matters. They are not wasteful.

26. Winners Are Always Improving

Winners make personal development a priority. And always try to improve for the better.

27. Winners Learn From Their Mistakes

Winners make a conscious effort to right their wrongs and learn from their experiences. They know that nobody's perfect but that it doesn't hurt to try.

***

It is my hope that something in this book has inspired you. I would like for you to take the next few moments and utilize the following pages in this book to write down the things that have held you back from swapping to the life you really want and what you plan to swap today forward in order to achieve it all. I'm a living witness that you can have whatever life you want to live. Period.

Dear Life,

_____
_____
_____
_____
_____
_____
_____
_____
_____
_____
_____
_____
_____
_____
_____
_____
_____
_____
_____
_____
_____
_____
_____
_____
_____
_____
_____

Online Resources/Citations

- **Business Insider**
- **Psychology Today**
- **Thought Catalog**
- **Bloomberg**
- **Huffington Post**
- **Tiny Buddha**
- **Personal Growth for Christians**
- **Sermon Central**
- **Growth Central**
- **Investopedia**